Let's Visit the Supermarket

Marianne Johnston

The Rosen Publishing Group's
PowerKids Press™
New York

Published in 2000 by The Rosen Publishing Group, Inc.
29 East 21st Street, New York, NY 10010

First Edition

Book design: Danielle Primiceri

Photo Credits:p. 4 © Uniphoto Picture Agency; p. 6 © Telegraph Colour Library/FPG International; p. 7 © Keystone View Co./FPG International; p. 8 © Daemmrich/The Image Works, Ron Chapple/FPG International; p. 11 © Charles Gupton/Uniphoto Picture Agency; p. 12 © M. Granitsas/The Image Works; p. 13 © Crandall Wray/The Image Works; p. 14 © Daniel Wray/The Image Works; p. 15 © Daemmrich/The Image Works; p. 16 © M. Antman/The Image Works; p. © Uniphoto Picture Agency; p. 20 © LLEWELLYN/Uniphoto Picture Agency; p. 21 © Barbara Peacock/FPG International.

Johnston, Marianne.
     Let's visit the supermarket / by Marianne Johnston.
          p.   cm. — (Our community)
     Includes index.
     Summary: Describes the roles of different workers in the supermarket, how supermarkets stock and store food, and why the supermarket is an important part of the community.
     ISBN 0-8239-5436-6 (lib. bdg.)
     1. Supermarkets Juvenile literature. [1. Supermarkets.] I. Title. II. Series: Johnston, Marianne. Our community.
     HF5469.J64   1999
     381'.148—dc21   99-20154
                                                                                                              CIP

Contents

Supermarkets in Our Communities

Do you ever wonder where all those thousands of items at the supermarket come from? A lot of work goes into getting that can of soup onto the shelf of your local supermarket. Supermarkets bring food from all over the country to your **community**.

The supermarket isn't just a place for people in our communities to buy food. It's a place for people in the community to come together. When you go to the supermarket with your parents, do you ever see your friends and neighbors there?

◄ *The thousands of items on the supermarket shelves come from all over the country, and the world!*

History of Supermarkets

Before the first supermarkets appeared, people went to different shops for different kinds of food. Butcher shops sold meat, bakeries sold bread, and vegetables were often sold from stands in outdoor markets. A man named Michael Cullen opened the first supermarket in 1930. The store was in New York City and it was named King Kullen. Mr. Cullen's store had all kinds of food under one roof.

People used to go to lots of different stores to get what they needed. ▶

How Supermarkets Work

Supermarkets have a few different **departments**, such as meat, **dairy**, grocery, and **produce**. A **manager** runs each department. The managers make sure their departments are filled with food.

Food from all over the country is shipped to a supermarket **chain's** main **warehouse**. People who work at the warehouse are in charge of buying food from the farms and food companies. They are called buyers. Each one of these warehouses stores tons of food to be delivered to nearby stores.

◀ *The supermarket has different departments for the different kinds of food it sells.*

Ordering Food From the Warehouse

Each morning, a manager uses an order machine to place an order to the warehouse. The order machine is a little computer that has a handle on the bottom and a small screen on the top. Each item sold in the supermarket has a code that the computer understands. If a manager needs 500 cans of peas for his department, he will scan the code for peas into the order machine, then punch in the number of cans he needs. This order is received by someone at the warehouse.

If an order is placed at 6:00 AM, it will usually arrive by about 4:00 PM. ▶

Here Come the Trucks

Three different kinds of trucks deliver food to supermarkets. Grocery trucks carry items such as canned soup, rice, and crackers. They are 18-wheel trucks that usually come to the supermarket once a day. **Refrigerated** trucks carry produce, meat, and dairy, and must be kept cool. Frozen-food trucks are kept at 0 degrees Fahrenheit, so items like frozen dinners and ice cream won't **defrost**.

FUN FACTS

Food is unloaded from the trucks at a docking bay at the back of the supermarket.

◀ *Workers unload all the food that comes to the supermarket.*

13

Behind the Scenes at the Supermarket

Have you ever wondered what is behind those swinging doors at the back of the supermarket? The doors open into a storage room where boxes of canned and packaged food are stored. The produce preparation room is also in the back. The **produce clerk** uses this room to wash and trim the vegetables and fruit so they look nice and fresh for the customers.

14

A lot of preparation goes into the foods you see at the supermarket. ▶

Refrigerators as Big as a Room

Can you imagine walking into a refrigerator? At the supermarket, foods like milk and frozen vegetables are taken directly from the delivery truck to huge refrigerators, called coolers. The produce, dairy, and meat coolers are found in the back of the supermarket. They are kept pretty cold at 34 degrees, just above freezing. These coolers usually have big steel doors that help keep in the cold air.

FUN FACTS

Many supermarkets are open 24 hours a day.

◀ *Meat is stored in a big refrigerator until it is put out in the display cooler.*

Keeping the Food Cool

Lots of the food in the supermarket must be kept cool, even while it is on display. The display cases for frozen food are kept at 0 degrees Fahrenheit. This way, the warm air that flows in when people open the doors won't cause the food to defrost.

The produce cases are also refrigerated. Fruits and vegetables would not last long on display if they were not kept cool. Colder air flows over the fruits and vegetables from the bottom of the case to the top to keep the produce cool.

The food in the frozen section of the supermarket ▶
would go bad if it wasn't refrigerated.

Cashiers and the Cash Register

The cashier checks customers out when they are ready to pay for their groceries. The machine that the cashier uses is called a cash register. The cash register has many different buttons and parts, including a **scanner**. The scanner understands the price codes of products. A cashier spends 8 to 12 hours learning how to use the cash register. Cash registers are connected to a computer that tracks what gets sold each day.

FUN FACTS

Many supermarkets sell almost 30,000 items each day.

The cashier runs items over the scanner to input prices.

Other People at the Supermarket

There are lots of different jobs at the supermarket. Grocery clerks make sure the store stays neat and clean. There are butchers to cut the meat, and produce clerks to clean and prepare the vegetables. All the workers at the supermarket help to make it an important part of the community.

Web Sites:

You can learn more about supermarkets on the Internet. Check out this Web site: http://www.mysupermarket.com

Glossary

chain (CHAYN) A group of stores in many different locations with the same name that are run by the same national company.

community (kuh-MYOO-nih-tee) A group of people who have something in common, such as a special interest or the area where they live.

dairy (DAY-ree) Foods such as milk, cheese, and yogurt that are made from milk products.

defrost (dih-FROST) When something that is frozen thaws out, or warms up.

department (dih-PART-ment) A section of the grocery store that sells a certain type of product, such as meat or produce.

manager (MAN-uh-jer) The person in charge of a department at the supermarket.

produce (PROH-doos) Vegetables and fruit at the supermarket.

produce clerks (PROH-doos KLERKS) The people who clean and wash the fruits and vegetables to get them ready to be sold.

refrigerated (ree-FRIH-jer-ay-ted) To keep something cold.

scanner (SKAN-er) The part of the cash register that reads the code on each item.

warehouse (WAIR-hows) The place where food from all over the country is stored until it is needed by local stores.

Index